Galations

Vaughn D. Reece

Copyright 2016 by Vaughn D. Reece.
The book author retains sole copyright to
his contributions to this book.
Published 2016.
Printed in the United States of America.

All rights reserved.

No portion of this book may be reproduced, stored in a retrieval system, or transmitted in any form or by any means – electronic, mechanical, photocopy, recording, scanning, or other – except for brief quotations in critical reviews or articles, without the prior written permission of the author.

ISBN 978-1-946234-01-8

Front cover design by Mark Gauthier.

This book was published by BookCrafters,
Parker, Colorado.
bookcrafterscolorado@gmail.com

This book may be ordered from
www.bookcrafters.net and other online bookstores.

Foreword

Thank you for selecting this volume of the Expository series. These volumes are the contribution of various Apostolic writers. Their biography is on the back cover. The publishers of the Expository series would like to extend a thank you for helping us get this valuable material into the hands of readers.

The desire is that people would read the scriptures and be blessed. These commentary works, or works of Expository subjects, will give insight to, and further the understanding of the readers.

Each of these authors hold the values of the original Apostles of Jesus Christ. These writers want to hold to the values expostulated in the New Testament by Jesus and his disciples. Each of them ascribe to the concept offered by the Apostle John, " I have no greater joy than to hear that my children walk in truth".

Truth has been passed down through generations and has survived critics and doubters. Truth will prevail and ultimately triumph.

These writings are our contribution to the river of written truth that has flowed down through the ages.

Read and be blessed.

Kenneth Bow

Introduction

Authorship:
The letter to the churches of Galatia is so clearly in the style and the methodology of Pauline thought that very few scholars throughout the centuries have questioned his authorship. Substantive portions of the letter's style, vocabulary and theology connects Apostle Paul as the author as well as the various personal references made in certain passages (1:1, 1:12-24, 5:2). The early church held a strong and unwavering belief that Apostle Paul was indeed the writer.

Recipients, Occasion and Timeframe:
Galatians is the only one of Paul's letters written and addressed to a group of churches rather than a single location. The epistle has been called a spiritual Magna Carta because of the scholarly and masterful exposition of our justification by faith.

The letter addressed to the churches of Galatia emphasizes the sufficiency of justification by obedient faith in the new birth salvation. This region had many Gentile converts in the early apostolic church and some were being taught the requirement to add certain Jewish rituals required under the law to their new found faith;

such as circumcision of the flesh. Paul calls them back to the gospel they have suddenly deserted (1:6). The new gospel they have embraced really is no gospel at all (1:7). The true gospel, the one Paul had preached, came through Jesus Christ by revelation directly to Paul (1:12). It is the same gospel preached by the other apostles (2:7-9). Paul rebuked the Galatian doctrinal error, pointing them again to Jesus. He knew what it was like to live under the law and he passionately and strongly defended our justification by obedient faith alone; in order to retain their spiritual freedom in Christ. This strengthening; and at times, very hard hitting; letter appears to have been written before AD 50; thus, making it one of the earliest New Testament letters

Theme:
The brief outline of Galatians is an introduction found in chapter 1:1-5. In chapters 1:6-2:14, Paul gives an articulate defense of his apostolic authority. In chapters 2:15-4:31, we are given his apostolic treatise on justification by obedient faith alone. In chapters 5:1-6:10, Paul skillfully and masterfully describes our Christian freedom and its related responsibilities; which must be embraced by the apostolic church. Finally, in chapter 6:10-18, we find his Pauline conclusion.

Chapter 1

1:1-5 Paul, an apostle, (not of men, neither by man, but by Jesus Christ, and God the Father, who raised him from the dead;) 2 And all the brethren which are with me, unto the churches of Galatia: 3 Grace be to you and peace from God the Father, and from our Lord Jesus Christ, 4 Who gave himself for our sins, that he might deliver us from this present evil world, according to the will of God and our Father: 5 To whom be glory for ever and ever. Amen.

1:1-5. Paul declares that his apostleship was not executed by a certain group or a fellow man, but exclusively by Almighty God who was manifested in the flesh as our Lord and Savior Jesus Christ. Paul, the apostle to the gentiles, received his apostleship directly from our resurrected, glorified, and exalted Jesus. The phrase of "He alone" points to Jesus rather than anyone else, and unmasks the underlying theological error at hand of salvation through their own effort under the law; for only the true gospel of the Lord Jesus Christ redeems and frees men and women from spiritual bondage.

1:6-7 I marvel that ye are so soon removed from him that called you into the grace of Christ unto another

gospel: 7 Which is not another; but there be some that trouble you, and would pervert the gospel of Christ.

1:6-7. The churches of Galatia are in the initial stages of deflecting from god and being deceived to receive a completely false gospel. The popular pseudo gospel is not the same one Paul preached. The apostolic new birth message of salvation differed drastically from the hybrid gospel preached and embraced by the legalists of Judaism.

1:8-10 But though we, or an angel from heaven, preach any other gospel unto you than that which we have preached unto you, let him be accursed. 9 As we said before, so say I now again, if any man preach any other gospel unto you than that ye have received, let him be accursed. 10 For do I now persuade men, or God? Or do I seek to please men? For if I yet pleased men, I should not be the servant of Christ.

1:8-10. Paul is declaring that sound doctrine is absolutely non-negotiable; hence, we see that the controversy at hand is not so much over preachers or personalities, but more importantly about embracing truth and rejecting error. Ultimately, the Truth of the Gospel is more important than the messenger who is delivering it; even if it involves an apostle. Furthermore, if false doctrine is delivered and preached by a celestial being, it must be rejected and the angel should be eternally condemned.

1:11-12 But I certify you, brethren, that the gospel which was preached of me is not after man. 12 For I neither received it of man, neither was I taught it, but by the revelation of Jesus Christ.

1:11-12. Paul's gospel is genuine, because prior to his direct revelation and conversion to the true gospel, he had sought only to destroy the Jesus Name message; but, with his Damascus road conversion he received the message of salvation directly from our risen Lord and Savior Jesus Christ.

1:13-24 For ye have heard of my conversation in time past in the Jews' religion, how that beyond measure I persecuted the church of God, and wasted it: 14 And profited in the Jews' religion above many my equals in mine own nation, being more exceedingly zealous of the traditions of my fathers. 15 But when it pleased God, who separated me from my mother's womb, and called me by his grace, 16 To reveal his Son in me, that I might preach him among the heathen; immediately I conferred not with flesh and blood: 17 Neither went I up to Jerusalem to them which were apostles before me, but I went into Arabia, and returned again unto Damascus. 18 Then after three years I went up to Jerusalem to see Peter, and abode with him fifteen days. 19 But other of the apostles saw I none, save James the Lord's brother. 20 Now the things which I write unto you, behold, before God, I lie not. 21 Afterwards I came into the regions of Syria and Cilicia; 22 And was unknown by face unto the churches of Judaea which were in Christ: 23 But they had heard only, That he which persecuted us in times past now preacheth the faith which once he destroyed. 24 And they glorified God in me.

1:13-24. Formerly, Paul was more passionate about advancing the requirements and traditions under the law in Judaism than any of his peers. He spent about three years in Arabia and he conferred deeply with God there. During these three years he was not taught by men but directly by God. Paul's return to Jerusalem as a Christian grounded in sound doctrine is described in the Acts of the Apostles 9:26-30. Barnabas helped assure the true believers in Jerusalem of Paul's conversion and new life; there he fellowshipped with Peter; and likely heard the eyewitness accounts of Jesus' earthly ministry and majesty.

Chapter 2

2:1-5 Then fourteen years after I went up again to Jerusalem with Barnabas, and took Titus with me also. 2 And I went up by revelation, and communicated unto them that gospel which I preach among the Gentiles, but privately to them which were of reputation, lest by any means I should run, or had run, in vain. 3 But neither Titus, who was with me, being a Greek, was compelled to be circumcised: 4 And that because of false brethren unawares brought in, who came in privily to spy out our liberty which we have in Christ Jesus, that they might bring us into bondage: 5 To whom we gave place by subjection, no, not for an hour; that the truth of the gospel might continue with you.

2:1-5. Luke in writing the Acts of the Apostles (11:29-30; 15:2) mentions two separate trips Paul and Barnabas made to Jerusalem. Fourteen years following his first visit to see Peter in Jerusalem (1:18), Paul made his second journey to Jerusalem this time with his fellow laborers Barnabas and Titus. In Jerusalem, Paul discoursed with John, James, and Peter regarding his God given apostleship to labor as a missionary to the Gentile world and to zealously preach the new birth apostolic message of salvation; without circumcision of the flesh; but rather, circumcision of the heart; on the basis of obedient faith in Christ. It is clearly evident to the early church that Paul was preaching the true gospel; divinely originated and natured. The same gospel was preached by the other apostles; and any other gospel of must be rejected. Not even angelic visions or a different version from Paul himself should entice the Galatians to exchange their original apostolic faith for another one.

2:6-14 But of these who seemed to be somewhat, (whatsoever they were, it maketh no matter to me: God accepteth no man's person:) for they who seemed to be somewhat in conference added nothing to me: 7 But contrariwise, when they saw that the gospel of the uncircumcision was committed unto me, as the gospel of the circumcision was unto Peter; 8 (For he that wrought effectually in Peter to the apostleship of the circumcision, the same was mighty in me toward the Gentiles:) 9 And when James, Cephas, and John, who seemed to be pillars, perceived the grace that was given unto me, they gave to me and Barnabas the right hands of fellowship; that we should go unto the heathen, and they unto the circumcision. 10 Only they would that we should remember the poor; the same which I also was forward to do. 11 But when Peter was come to Antioch, I withstood him to the face, because he was to be blamed. 12 For before that certain came from James, he did eat with the Gentiles: but when they were come, he withdrew and separated himself, fearing them which were of the circumcision. 13 And the other Jews dissembled likewise with him; insomuch that Barnabas also was carried away with their dissimulation. 14 But when I saw that

they walked not uprightly according to the truth of the gospel, I said unto Peter before them all, If thou, being a Jew, livest after the manner of Gentiles, and not as do the Jews, why compellest thou the Gentiles to live as do the Jews?

2:6-14. Paul submitted his gospel to the apostles for their unified endorsement. They acknowledged his gospel to be genuine and to be the same gospel they preached. The apostles gave him and Barnabas the right hand of fellowship affirming Paul and Barnabas as fellow laborers in Gospel of our Lord Jesus Christ. Paul rebuked requiring the rituals of the Law on Christians and any attempt to pervert the truth of the gospel. He realized that they all had their respective callings to attend to; however, they must all preach the same unadulterated gospel to fulfil their callings blamelessly. The Christians in Jerusalem were upset about the Christians in Antioch eating forbidden foods. Paul confronts Peter publicly and challenges his attitudes and actions for forcing the Gentile Christians to become Jewish proselytes.

2:15-21 We who are Jews by nature, and not sinners of the Gentiles, 16 Knowing that a man is not justified by the works of the law, but by the faith of Jesus Christ, even we have believed in Jesus Christ, that we might be justified by the faith of Christ, and not by the works of the law: for by the works of the law shall no flesh be justified. 17 But if, while we seek to be justified by Christ, we ourselves also are found sinners, is therefore Christ the minister of sin? God forbid. 18 For if I build again the things which I destroyed, I make myself a transgressor. 19 For I through the law am dead to the law, that I might live unto God. 20 I am crucified with Christ: nevertheless I live; yet not

I, but Christ liveth in me: and the life which I now live in the flesh I live by the faith of the Son of God, who loved me, and gave himself for me. 21 I do not frustrate the grace of God: for if righteousness come by the law, then Christ is dead in vain.

2:15-21. The Jewish Christians understood that a person can only be justified by obedient faith in Christ; that is, to be accounted by God as acceptable to Him. The Jewish legalists' objection to the doctrine of justification by obedient faith alone followed to its ultimate logical conclusion, would conversely make Jesus Christ the minister of sin. Thus, Apostle Paul emphatically and rightly declares, God forbid! He demanded that they deny such false teaching rooted in error. Paul has died to sin, in essence that is, he has died to the law as a means of justification and peace with God. In other words, Paul died to the self-righteousness that come from knowing the letter of the law versus knowing the Spirit of Christ; the Holy Ghost; which brings resurrection power to the believer in obedient faith. Thus, we find that Christ fulfilled the law, and delivered him from sin. By justification through obedient faith, the message is that apostolic believers are set free from sin and empowered to serve and glorify Jesus Christ. Paul declares that I no longer live, but Christ lives in me. Since, the apostolic believer is freed from the law and sin, the old sinful life should no longer assert itself; but rather, the Holy Ghost dwelling within the apostolic believer should assert Himself and bring forth newness of life saturated in resurrection power: i.e., the fruit, the character, the mind and the power of the Resurrected Christ.

Chapter 3

3:1-5 O foolish Galatians, who hath bewitched you, that ye should not obey the truth, before whose eyes Jesus Christ hath been evidently set forth, crucified among you? 2 This only would I learn of you, Received ye the Spirit by the works of the law, or by the hearing of faith? 3 Are ye so foolish? having begun in the Spirit, are ye now made perfect by the flesh? 4 Have ye suffered so many things in vain? If it be yet in vain. 5 He therefore that ministereth to you the Spirit, and worketh miracles among you, doeth he it by the works of the law, or by the hearing of faith?

3:1-5. When Paul originally preached and taught the gospel to the Galatians, they were given spiritual revelation and clear understanding of the apostolic message. However, now they were becoming spiritually confused; and not remaining steadfast in their obedience to the gospel of our Lord Jesus Christ. So Paul intentionally works tirelessly to expound truth and leave no middle ground between justification by faith and justification by works. He declares that the true gospel must solely rely upon the justification of obedient faith in Jesus Christ, and never by the works of the law. Paul appeals to the Galatians' own spiritual experience to argue salvation by obedient faith. The apostle refers to the Spirit in their new birth experience. When one is born again of the water and of the Spirit, he or she will receive the gift of the Holy Ghost (John 3:1-8, 4:10-14, 7:37-39; Acts 2:38-39). Paul states that they received the Spirit not by the works of the law, but by the obedience of faith. That new life which they have begun in the Power of the Spirit is a continual calling to growth in the Christian life. Galatian brothers and sisters are admonished to not forget that God poured out the Holy Ghost and worked miracles among the churches in Galatia; as a result of their unfeigned and obedient faith.

3:6-14 Even as Abraham believed God, and it was accounted to him for righteousness. 7 Know ye therefore that they which are of faith, the same are the children of Abraham. 8 And the scripture, foreseeing that God would justify the heathen through faith, preached before the gospel unto Abraham, saying, In thee shall all nations be blessed. 9 So then they which be of faith are blessed with faithful Abraham. 10 For as many as are of the works of the law are under the curse: for it is written, Cursed is every one that continueth not in all things which are written in the book of the law to do them. 11 But that no man is justified by the law in the sight of God, it is evident: for, The just shall live by faith. 12 And the law is not of faith: but, The man that doeth them shall live in them. 13 Christ hath redeemed us from the curse of the law, being made a curse for us: for it is written, Cursed is every one that hangeth on a tree: 14 That the blessing of Abraham might come on the Gentiles through Jesus Christ; that we might receive the promise of the Spirit through faith.

3:6-14. Paul communicates that scripture declares that Abraham's faith justified him and produced an example in the Patriarch's life of continued obedience. Father Abraham stands as an example to the Old and New Testament, natural Jew and spiritual Jew. Paul continues to make the case in addition to referring to the Galatians' own experience by now making his appeal to Old Testament Scripture. The Galatians received God's Spirit by obedient faith as Abraham received God's Righteousness by obedient faith (Gen. 15:6). All who were under the curse can now avoid the punishment of sin; to be under the curse is to be subject to God's wrath and condemnation. Perfect obedience to the law is impossible (Acts 15:10; James 2:10). The Holy Ghost is God's earnest payment of our eternal inheritance; it is the source of power by which apostolic believers are empowered to live new lives in Christ. This justification is the covenant blessing of Father Abraham, which Paul has been describing.

3:15-18 Brethren, I speak after the manner of men; Though it be but a man's covenant, yet if it be confirmed, no man disannulleth, or addeth thereto. 16 Now to Abraham and his seed were the promises made. He saith not, And to seeds, as of many; but as of one, And to thy seed, which is Christ. 17 And this I say, that the covenant, that was confirmed before of God in Christ, the law, which was four hundred and thirty years after, cannot disannul, that it should make the promise of none effect. 18 For if the inheritance be of the law, it is no more of promise: but God gave it to Abraham by promise.

3:15-18. Paul uses the argument based on the nature of covenants. He continues to make his case by now also appealing to the Abrahamic covenant. After God made a covenant with Abraham, He was not going to renege. And God's promise wasn't just to Abraham but included all of his descendants as well. The law, coming 430 years later, could not negate the covenant nor the promises ratified by God.

3:19-24 Wherefore then serveth the law? It was added because of transgressions, till the seed should come to whom the promise was made; and it was ordained by angels in the hand of a mediator. 20 Now a mediator is not a mediator of one, but God is one. 21 Is the law then against the promises of God? God forbid: for if there had been a law given which could have given life, verily righteousness should have been by the law. 22 But the scripture hath concluded all under sin, that the promise by faith of Jesus Christ might be given to them that believe. 23 But before faith came, we were kept under the law, shut up unto the faith which should afterwards be revealed. 24 Wherefore the law was our schoolmaster to bring us unto Christ, that we might be justified by faith.

3:19-24. He continues to make his case by now also appealing to the purpose of the law. The purpose of the Law being added was necessary because of the sin of mankind. The law made clear God's standard, and when man overstepped it, he became guilty of transgression. Paul declares that the law came at a later date and did not supersede or set aside the promise of justification by faith. And although there are differences between law and promises the two are not opposed in God's plan. The law proved our sinful condition and served to teach us and ultimately, in God's perfect timeline, the law helped lead us to

Christ; who is the only perfect work of redemption for the Jew and Gentile's sinful condition.

3:25-29 But after that faith is come, we are no longer under a schoolmaster. 26 For ye are all the children of God by faith in Christ Jesus. 27 For as many of you as have been baptized into Christ have put on Christ. 28 There is neither Jew nor Greek, there is neither bond nor free, there is neither male nor female: for ye are all one in Christ Jesus. 29 And if ye be Christ's, then are ye Abraham's seed, and heirs according to the promise.

3:25-29. Judaism in many ways was a religion of exclusion; Paul's point here is that the true Gospel of Jesus Christ breaks down all exclusionary barriers; such as Jews, Gentiles, slaves, free men or women, etc. – and thus, allowing equal access to God's presence and salvation for all of God's creation; regardless of their race or social status. In our new birth salvation and in the converted life to the true Gospel, we are no longer forced to live under the curse of the law; because thanks be to Christ, the law has actually fulfilled its purpose in Jesus Christ.

Chapter 4

4:1-31. Paul continues to strengthen the argument of his treatise on justification by obedient faith in Jesus Christ, and not as a result of justification of works; keeping the law. Paul articulates his final systematic points by appealing to the law's temporary nature (4:1-11), and by the powerful allegory laid out (4:22-31).

4:1-7 Now I say, That the heir, as long as he is a child, differeth nothing from a servant, though he be lord of all; 2 But is under tutors and governors until the time appointed of the father. 3 Even so we, when we were children, were in bondage under the elements of the world: 4 But when the fulness of the time was come, God sent forth his Son, made of a woman, made under the law, 5 To redeem them that were under the law, that we might receive the adoption of sons. 6 And because ye are sons, God hath sent forth the Spirit of his Son into your hearts, crying, Abba, Father. 7 Wherefore thou art no more a servant, but a son; and if a son, then an heir of God through Christ.

4:1-7. Apostle Paul is referring to the Roman guardianship of children under age to teach man that man is no longer subject to keeping the law. It was quite common for wealthy Roman fathers to appoint guardians for the management of his child's legal affairs until the heir came of age. Hence, the metaphor is that the old period of spiritual immaturity under the law is now compared against the Christian's newly received freedom in Christ. Oftentimes, tutors would rule over the underage offspring and/or the government would temporarily rule over their assets. Likewise, in times past, as God's offspring we were subject to elementary religious teachings and practices prior to the full measure of Christ; it was not yet time for us to become spiritually mature sons. However, when the fullness of the time came; God was manifested in the flesh. He came under the law in order to fulfill it and set free those under the under the mandatory tutorship of the law. Thus, it is through our Lord and Savior Jesus Christ; God manifested in the flesh; that every apostolic believer becomes God's son or daughter by the new birth experience. And every true spiritual child of God is adopted by Him when they are justified by faith and receive the gift of the Holy Ghost; this Spirit of adoption brings the blessed assurance that God is our Abba Father. Thus, we are no longer servants to the law; and as sons of God, we are powerfully admonished to grow into the full measure of Christ.

4:8–21 Howbeit then, when ye knew not God, ye did service unto them which by nature are no gods. 9 But now, after that ye have known God, or rather are known of God, how turn ye again to the weak and beggarly elements, whereunto ye desire again to be in bondage? 10 Ye observe days, and months, and times, and years. 11 I am afraid of you, lest I have bestowed upon you labour in vain. 12 Brethren, I beseech you, be as I am; for I am as ye are: ye have not injured me

at all. 13 Ye know how through infirmity of the flesh I preached the gospel unto you at the first. 14 And my temptation which was in my flesh ye despised not, nor rejected; but received me as an angel of God, even as Christ Jesus. 15 Where is then the blessedness ye spake of? for I bear you record, that, if it had been possible, ye would have plucked out your own eyes, and have given them to me. 16 Am I therefore become your enemy, because I tell you the truth? 17 They zealously affect you, but not well; yea, they would exclude you, that ye might affect them. 18 But it is good to be zealously affected always in a good thing, and not only when I am present with you. 19 My little children, of whom I travail in birth again until Christ be formed in you, 20 I desire to be present with you now, and to change my voice; for I stand in doubt of you. 21 Tell me, ye that desire to be under the law, do ye not hear the law?

4:8-21. Prior to the Galatians' new birth experience, they served the gods of this world; however, now they serve the Lord Jesus Christ. The Mosaic Law could not save and was inferior to the New Covenant. Thus, by the Galatians embracing the Old Covenant of salvation by works, it would negate their declaration of freedom under the new and better covenant in the apostolic faith. Paul continues his appeal to be set free indeed by the truth of Jesus Christ. He demonstrates his confidence that the Galatians were still thankful to have been saved under his ministry. So Paul appeals to this deep love as their father in the Gospel to reject the false teachers slipping in among the churches of Galatia. Those false teachers are actually dangerous heretics set out to cause great division between them and Paul. However, the beloved apostle reminds them that his love is genuine and that has their best interest at heart; Paul is sacrificially laboring so they will grow in the grace and knowledge of Jesus Christ and become mature apostolic believers; steadfast and unmovable.

4:22-31 For it is written, that Abraham had two sons, the one by a bondmaid, the other by a freewoman. 23 But he who was of the bondwoman was born after the flesh; but he of the freewoman was by promise. 24 Which things are an allegory: for these are the two covenants; the one from the mount Sinai, which gendereth to bondage, which is Agar. 25 For this Agar is mount Sinai in Arabia, and answereth to Jerusalem which now is, and is in bondage with her children. 26 But Jerusalem which is above is free, which is the mother of us all. 27 For it is written, Rejoice, thou barren that bearest not; break forth and cry, thou that travailest not: for the desolate hath many more children than she which hath an husband. 28 Now we, brethren, as Isaac was, are the children of promise. 29 But as then he that was born after the flesh persecuted him that was born after the Spirit, even so it is now. 30 Nevertheless what saith the scripture? Cast out the bondwoman and her son: for the son of the bondwoman shall not be heir with the son of the freewoman. 31 So then, brethren, we are not children of the bondwoman, but of the free.

4:22-31. Paul articulates this last appeal by a powerful allegory; we must always remember that Ishmael was born to a slave-woman by absolute human efforts; on the other hand, Isaac was born to a free-woman by absolute divine promise (Gen. 16:15; 21:2). In this powerful picture, Paul is masterfully connecting Hagar to the bondage of the old covenant; the one with less followers. On the other hand, the followers of Christ are being connected to the New Jerusalem; the heavenly city. Thus, the apostolic church is not under the servitude of the law; and furthermore, it is certain, that as heirs of the promise; the apostolic church; born of the new covenant; will have many more followers of Christ. Paul clearly communicates that the apostolic believers are born of divine promise; and this position of promise is only experienced through faith. Therefore, the Galatians are strongly and passionately beseeched to reject all heretical attempts to convert them to any pseudo gospel; which essentially attempts to require both justification by works (bondage) and justification by faith (freedom); they are mutually exclusive in the position of promise.

Chapter 5

5.1-26. Apostle Paul declares that the churches of Galatia must stand fast in the true liberty of the apostolic message; he sounds a concern to never willingly abuse their new liberty of Christ; and he proceeds to clearly identify numerous sinful practices and problem areas; while admonishing and provoking them to bearing the Spirit's fruit of blameless and godly works; only made possible through the Power of the Holy Ghost residing in their lives; as a result of the commonly shared and priceless new birth experience.

5:1-6 Stand fast therefore in the liberty wherewith Christ hath made us free, and be not entangled again with the yoke of bondage. 2 Behold, I Paul say unto you, that if ye be circumcised, Christ shall profit you nothing. 3 For I testify again to every man that is circumcised, that he is a debtor to do the whole law. 4 Christ is become of no effect unto you, whosoever of you are justified by the law; ye are fallen from grace. 5 For we through the Spirit wait for the hope of righteousness by faith. 6 For in Jesus Christ neither circumcision availeth any thing, nor uncircumcision; but faith which worketh by love.

5.1-6. Essentially, the beloved apostle emphatically teaches the Galatians that if they do not stand steadfastly and unmovable in the freedom of the truth and the way of Jesus Christ, they will prove it to become completely unprofitable in their own lives; thereby, losing their pure faith and joy of salvation and pointlessly putting on the old yoke of bondage in attempting to resurrect the ceremonial aspects of the law; which have been completely fulfilled in Jesus Christ. Hence, it is shameful for them to go back to the beggarly elements they had relinquished; and to not remain in the true faith of Christ.

5:7-18 Ye did run well; who did hinder you that ye should not obey the truth? 8 This persuasion cometh not of him that calleth you. 9 A little leaven leaveneth the whole lump. 10 I have confidence in you through the Lord, that ye will be none otherwise minded: but he that troubleth you shall bear his judgment, whosoever he be. 11 And I, brethren, if I yet preach circumcision, why do I yet suffer persecution? then is the offence of the cross ceased. 12 I would they were even cut off which trouble you. 13 For, brethren, ye have been called unto liberty; only use not liberty for an occasion to the flesh, but by love serve one another. 14 For all the law is fulfilled in one word, even in this; Thou shalt love thy neighbour as thyself. 15 But if ye bite and devour one another, take heed that ye be not consumed one of another. 16 This I say then, Walk in the Spirit, and ye shall not fulfil the lust of the flesh. 17 For the flesh lusteth against the Spirit, and the Spirit against the flesh: and these are contrary the one to the other: so that ye cannot do the things that ye would. 18 But if ye be led of the Spirit, ye are not under the law.

5:7-18. The Judaizers had confused them with a pseudo message; to such a degree that some of the Galatians were now refusing to obey the Truth of Jesus Christ; since the defense might come forth that the point of disagreement should be overlooked since it only involved a minor portion of the ceremonial law embraced and only by a few persons, the beloved apostle refers to a sound proverb: a little leaven leavens the whole lump. We can make no room or compromise for doctrinal error. Paul disputes the rumors that he also still preaches a gospel of circumcision, as formerly in Judaism. He removes this confusion by logically concluding that if that were truly the case, he would not be facing such direct offense and persecution from the Judaizers. Paul then conveys how that he desires for those false teachers; who are confusing the Galatian churches with their malignant doctrines; to be cut off by the Lord and the church. Apostolic Christians are not set free in order to abuse their liberty from the law and then walk unrestrained in their sinful nature. We are called into this freedom to serve God and one another blamelessly in the Body of Christ. Thus, he challenges them to always walk in the Spirit, whose fruit is love, and in doing so; they will not fulfil the lust of the flesh. Therefore, as they prayerfully live and walk in the Power of the Spirit they will be empowered to forsake their own fleshly and contrary natural desires and freely submit to the indwelling Holy Ghost and walk in humble submission; this is the only way apostolic believers are able to live victoriously over the works of the flesh in a God-pleasing manner. We have the assurance that every apostolic believer who lives by the Spirit will not carry out the desires their old sinful nature; for they oppose each other and cannot co-exist. Hence, the necessary outcome is that every

Christian must be led by the Spirit, and turn away from the flesh's evil yearnings; thus, putting sin out of his daily life. The Spirit-ruled person is not ruled under the temporal law because his lifestyle is ruled by the eternal Spirit.

5:19-26 Now the works of the flesh are manifest, which are these; Adultery, fornication, uncleanness, lasciviousness, 20 Idolatry, witchcraft, hatred, variance, emulations, wrath, strife, seditions, heresies, 21 Envyings, murders, drunkenness, revellings, and such like: of the which I tell you before, as I have also told you in time past, that they which do such things shall not inherit the kingdom of God. 22 But the fruit of the Spirit is love, joy, peace, longsuffering, gentleness, goodness, faith, 23 Meekness, temperance: against such there is no law. 24 And they that are Christ's have crucified the flesh with the affections and lusts. 25 If we live in the Spirit, let us also walk in the Spirit. 26 Let us not be desirous of vain glory, provoking one another, envying one another.

5:19-26. Apostle Paul now contrasts the works of the flesh with the fruit of the Spirit. True believers in Christ are led by his Spirit, and they bear the evidential fruit of it; thereby, they have crucified the flesh and its lusts by the indwelling power of the Holy Ghost. Paul's list of sins appears to address four problem areas: the first three terms are sexual or immoral, the next two are false gods, the next eight are various sins of personal conflict, and the final two are sins of drunkenness. It also appears that rather than being a complete of all sins, this is really a list of the pressing problem areas within the churches of Galatia. (For example the list is similar to other lists provided in other letters to the early Apostolic Church found in 1 Cor. 5:9-11; 6:9-10; 2 Cor. 12:20-21; 1 Tim. 1:9-10. Every apostolic believer must grow into the full measure of Christ and face the facts whether he is walking by the Spirit or being controlled by the flesh. In the true Freedom of Christ; there is no allowance for any form of deviant and sexual lifestyle sins; all forms of idolatry are evil and sinful, they lead to spiritual bondage and are absolutely forbidden. In the true Freedom of Christ; we will not worship any object or person; we cannot afford to fool with the powers of the destructive occult world. In the true Freedom of Christ; we cannot afford to walk in evil strife, discord, jealousy or egotistical and selfish ambitions; or to become confused with evil dissensions and doctrinal heresies; we cannot afford to yield our flesh to uncontrolled revelings in purely excessive gluttonous and carousing lifestyles; and thereby bringing shameful disgrace upon the power and freedom of Christ. Any believer willingly and unrepentantly living in those sins will not inherit the kingdom of God, because he or she is not ruled by the Spirit of Christ; those who freely do such things are none of Christ's. True believers in Christ are led by his Spirit, and will bear the evidential and mature fruit of it; granted as fruit on a tree takes time to grow and mature, so the Spirit does not cultivate these virtues in the believer's life overnight. Nonetheless, we must bear the evidential fruit of willingly and sacrificially giving of ourselves in love for the Kingdom of God; we must bear the evidential fruit of living with gladness of heart; living with: tranquility of mind, free from worry and fear; having patience with others, not being short tempered; having kindness and generosity; having dependability and gentleness in relations with others;

and by having self-control, harnessing evil passions and lusts. Finally, the beloved apostle concludes this powerful discourse with the assurance that every true believer will turn renounce the old life of sin and live by the Spirit.

Chapter 6

6:1-6 Brethren, if a man be overtaken in a fault, ye which are spiritual, restore such an one in the spirit of meekness; considering thyself, lest thou also be tempted. 2 Bear ye one another's burdens, and so fulfil the law of Christ. 3 For if a man think himself to be something, when he is nothing, he deceiveth himself. 4 But let every man prove his own work, and then shall he have rejoicing in himself alone, and not in another. 5 For every man shall bear his own burden. 6 Let him that is taught in the word communicate unto him that teacheth in all good things.

6:1-6. Apostle Paul appears to be describing sin, which involves intentional disobedience of God's commandments. The members of the church who were strong in the Spirit of God, in other words those who have been faithfully living and walking in the Spirit, and standing steadfast by the power and grace of the Holy Ghost, are called to restore the erring brother. However, those working to bring restoration must keep praying and watching diligently over their own lives. So Paul admonishes to help and provide relief from the burdens, and when doing so we literally make others' griefs and sorrows our own; thus, the law of Christ is working and we are following His example set in scriptures; this is a powerful example authentic Apostolic Christianity. It is dangerous for a man to think of himself as incapable of moral failure; or better than others; furthermore, this type of man will tend to give less compassion and empathy in the failures of others; however, we must all decrease so that Christ may be increased in our lives. In order to avoid the self-deception of comparing our own moral life with the open faults of our brothers and sisters, we must humbly and prayerfully examine our own life and works; by the rule of God's word.

6:7-11 Be not deceived; God is not mocked: for whatsoever a man soweth, that shall he also reap. 8 For he that soweth to his flesh shall of the flesh reap corruption; but he that soweth to the Spirit shall of the Spirit reap life everlasting. 9 And let us not be weary in well doing: for in due season we shall reap, if we faint not. 10 As we have therefore opportunity, let us do good unto all men, especially unto them who are of the household of faith. 11 Ye see how large a letter I have written unto you with mine own hand.

6:7-11. To disobey God's commands and escape divine punishment would be to outsmart God, thus making a mockery of Him and His Word. Whatsoever a man sows, that shall he also reap; is a proverbial expression, which may be applied to all actions, good and bad, and the reward and punishment of them, and the lasting fruits. Men may deceive themselves, and others, with false appearances, yet they cannot ever deceive God, for God knows their hearts. The man who sows to his flesh is one that caters to his flesh, gratifies and indulges the vile lusts of it; he is one who lives after the corruption of the flesh doing the works of it and spending his life solely upon himself; the man whose whole sole identity is one of increasing worldly riches and self-exaltation; while forsaking his own soul, and forsaking the apostolic church family and the ministers of the Gospel. But he that sows to the Spirit is the person who sows spiritual things; and yields obediently to the things of the Spirit, daily living and walking in the Holy Ghost; this type of man will received eternal life. Apostolic believers are urged to take advantage of every opportunity to do good; first: they are charged to serve them who are of the apostolic faith; and second, to the rest of the world.

6:12-18 As many as desire to make a fair shew in the flesh, they constrain you to be circumcised; only lest they should suffer persecution for the cross of Christ. 13 For neither they themselves who are circumcised keep the law; but desire to have you circumcised, that they may glory in your flesh. 14 But God forbid that I should glory, save in the cross of our Lord Jesus Christ, by whom the world is crucified unto me, and I unto the world. 15 For in Christ Jesus neither circumcision availeth any thing, nor uncircumcision, but a new creature. 16 And as many as walk according to this rule, peace be on them, and mercy, and upon the Israel of God. 17 From henceforth let no man trouble me: for I bear in my body the marks of the Lord Jesus. 18 Brethren, the grace of our Lord Jesus Christ be with your spirit. Amen.

6:12-18. The false apostles, desired to outwardly appear righteous before men, and being accounted by them. The gospel was more likely to be tolerated by orthodox Jews if it added the requirement of circumcision and obedience to their law. So the false apostles, wanted to hold to the gospel, and disarm Jewish hostility by preaching both. But Paul had willingly renounced his old life and all of its ways, including the religious accomplishments in which he used to boast of in the flesh. In God's sight the external circumcision of the flesh produced no spiritual benefit under the new covenant. Unlike the false apostles, Paul bears bodily marks, which have meaning and value while living in the new covenant. Paul's marks are the wounds incurred in serving God, the results of having willingly accepted the persecution for the cross; which the false apostles avoided. In his concluding remark, the beloved apostle demonstrates his humility by putting the Galatians on the same level with himself; which the arrogant false teachers would never do; it is notable that Paul does not pray for the righteousness of works under the law be with them, but rather most importantly for the Grace of our Lord Jesus Christ to be upon them; that is in other words, for their ability to do God's will.

www.ingramcontent.com/pod-product-compliance
Lightning Source LLC
Chambersburg PA
CBHW040418100526
44588CB00022B/2868